VARIATIONS

on a Theme of Desire

SAINT JULIAN PRESS

POETRY SERIES

Variations on a Theme of Desire, David-Glen Smith's long-awaited first book, is the work of a mature, patient poet. Following in the footsteps of Walt Whitman, Mark Doty, Sylvia Plath, Lynda Hull, among many others, Smith wows the reader with his surprising imagery as he takes us on his erotic journey. In a section of "broken sonnets," he imagines telling an ex-lover about his current lover, "his beauty is like a fine, dense rain,/as a flood of levees, drowning out the horizon line—" Yet, he is still haunted by "impressions remaining from fingertips once pressed....The moment still drenches." Full of Biblical and mythological references, the book's back and forth movement includes dances with Death, metamorphosis and transcendence, ultimately, acceptance and forgiveness. Its complexity and beauty will entice the reader back again and again.

—Joan Seliger Sidney, *Body of Diminishing Motion* and *Bereft and Blessed*

David-Glen Smith's *Variations on a Theme of Desire* is equal parts philosophical text, archeological exploration, fairy tale, and map of human memory. It's no surprise a book of such grand scope sees saints of music, poetry, and faith appear in its pages. These are poems of jazz and crow, of the long dead and the just living, of the topography of a dreamscape built from the bones of those who walk, briefly or lingering, across our lives. But perhaps more than anything, this book is a guide written by a poet to his young son, something the boy can tuck away so that one day, when he's ready and capable of understanding, he can read and know the map of his father's heart. How, no matter the songs that play, the lyrics just underneath the melodies say, "Remember, son, in all aspects of this fragmented world—I will never leave you."

—Bryan Borland, author of *Less Fortunate Pirates*

Variations on a Theme of Desire

Poems

By

David-Glen Smith

Saint Julian Press

Houston

Published by Saint Julian Press, Inc.

2053 Cortlandt, Suite 200

Houston, Texas 77008

www.saintjulianpress.com

ISBN-13: 978-0-9889447-8-7

ISBN: 0-9889447-8-2

Library of Congress Control Number: 2015934003

Cover art is titled "Tread" by artist
Keith Perelli from New Orleans, LA.
www.keithperelli.com.

A nod to the past, to the present and to the upcoming future.

To Brendan, who came after the poems, who sketches crescents in sand.
To Ricky who remains my constant.

To my Mother, who gave me the value of language.
To my Father, who provided me the value of history.

To my Grandmother, who quietly understood.
For my brother Lane, who walks with blue horses.

— and to all others in my family.

TABLE OF CONTENTS

It is as if we have all been lowered into an atmosphere of glass.
Now and then a remark trails through the glass.
Ann Carson, "The Glass Essay"

Gather up the fragments that remain, that nothing be lost.
KJV, John 6:12

VARIATIONS

on a Theme of Desire

Section 1: Venerations of the Temple

The words left out of the poem are sacred.
                    —Yannis Ritsos
                    Monochords, trans. Paul Merchant

I heard what was said of the universe,
Heard it and heard it of several thousand years;
It is middling well as far as it goes— but is that all?
                    —Walt Whitman
                    Song of Myself, ll. 1023-1025

Twenty-Nine Reflections over the Remnants of a Codex
Left Behind by Saint Aidan, circa 620CE

These temple doors were once firmly closed.

Forgotten, the temple lies in ruins.

Along the altar, between tiles, a rush of panic grass grows in abundance.

Within the core of every human lies a hidden temple, a building rashly built—
without a door or entranceway.

The key is to build your own entry.

There was a time the temple within was locked. There was the moment you
reopened the temple doors for me.

A cupped hand over the heart constructs a temple; a fist over the heart builds
a wall.

Within the *Codex of Aidan*, a prophet comments how a single stone can begin
the building of any cathedral.

Even in a stone field, with only the voices of gathering crows, a temple exists.

The shadow of a temple creates its own cathedral.

The temple rests in disrepair, but wildflowers scatter across the stone gateway.

Seven stones lead to the front door from the eastern gateway—

Standing alone within the temple— myself and a few candles—

—the temple falls into silence—

Within the pulsing light of a hummingbird splintering time, within the depth
of its racing wild heart, a miniature cathedral is built, a temple with
hundreds of multiple rooms, each chamber and every niche complete
with a devotional shrine to an unknown Saint and forgotten Martyr
from antiquity, containing a miniscule tallow candle burning throughout
the night.

The child ringing a bell at the altar in a darkening church at twilight.

The cornerstone boulder fractures over time, but the Seal of the Seven
Founders remains visible: an open magnolia centered within an
equilateral triangle.

—in the manner psalms fracture in translation, meanings blurred over time
and generations—

Spanish missionaries once crossed this territory, centuries ago, bearing a cedar
box holding a braided lock of golden hair, a preserved icon of Mary
Magdalene traveling from the Old World to the New, sheltered by a
small band of monks seeking an undisclosed region to begin the
construction of their church—

What I mean to say is that a hummingbird by itself is a temple— all wings
fracturing the air, shifting time streams with machineries of joy,

—an affirmation of existence appears with the stroke of a match into fire, fire
against wick, the altar transforming into mosaic— diverse interpretations
of the word, of the text—
—realities reordered through observation, revisions of the text, within the
temples, text as identity, perception.
—outside the temple doors, in early morning, hummingbirds convene among
flowering canna lilies, scattered milkweed.
The sacred head of a sleeping child.
Graphite scratched across fresh paper, vellum, or even papyrus— establishes
the landscape of an idea, the perimeters of a psalm unfolding in new
light—
Fragments of psalms lingering, the burned Codex half ash, half ancestral
memory—
—as in a division, a segment removed, a chapter lifted from the main source,
temporarily put aside,
—or even physical distances repaired, the manner a fraction of sunlight shifts
up a cathedral's nave, a slow enveloping gesture taking in all aspects of
the whole.
—until a time when the various aspects can be refused, reunited, made whole.
The full selection of verses stitched back, slowly,

Twenty-Six Verses from an Apocryphal Psalm

1/ The psalm of a moment lies on the tongues of children,

2/ a moment fractured between acceptance and denial— the manner green-
acorn shells crunch underfoot, the water-oak a parable unto itself,

3/ or as a blood cypress burning in autumn, acting as a psalm unto itself,
as a child transforms to prayer or to papyrus, a folded page with
forgotten language,

4/ or a psalm of confusion, a confession (Events other than the ordinary
bring you to your knees.)

5/ or a psalm of confusion opening up as a prayer, fractured; faith as a ruined
building in a field of pale pampas grass.

6/ Every child is an untranslatable psalm. We try reading them at night by
dim lamps, wanting to build a charm of security over their sleeping
forms. All we can hope for is the prayers to reach a quiet heaven,
to remove the stains of our greatest fears—

7/ a torn envelope, for instance, with a scrawled name, illegible, in dark red
ink, as a reminder. A misplaced set of car keys. Piles of books waiting to
be re-shelved. A task now forgotten, mundane.

8/ Every child exists within a book of psalms: worn binding and stained
leather cover, with numerous dog-eared pages.

9/ Children's palms tremble sometimes, when holding a holy text, their
shadows slipping slowly over pages, shivering with God's full weight.

10/ Fractured psalms translate to children's voices— the pitch of phrases
caught in the wind, fragmented across distance, broken

11/ lines of their discourse becoming scraps of prayers— but then we are
caught unprepared for disaster, for sudden inexplicable moments—

12/ When we hold our child, we support him as a holy text, a book of
reverence, a book of hours, his body bound by our hands,

13/ by the definitions we establish, prayers we utter at night on bent knees
seeking a faith, a stronghold in darkness—

14/ or then, as a procession of children casting down fresh palm branches in
church aisles, the trembling, narrow descent of green

15/ —even light trembles for a moment before a candle is lit, as we tremble
in darkness at prospects of the world, as we watch a sleeping child.

16/ —we collect worries together in our palms as a gathering of pebbles, each
a psalm onto itself.

17/ A moment of hesitation always opens before a closed clinic door,
locked security windows;

18/ —for a moment of hesitation exists within motions of a drawer pulled open for
   proper parental identification;
19/ —for a moment of hesitation lies among cut blossoms gathered in a glass
   vase— when a name shatters into filaments of loss on tiles of the floor;
20/ —for here are items which remain:
   the shadow of an indentation along the curve of a pillow,
   the cusp of motion shifting a foot into a shoe,
   the slight fall and rise of a backyard swing caught in a breath of wind;
21/ —for here are items which are gained:
   the curved form of your partner weeping on the corner of the bed,
   faith as a stone in the pit of your stomach,
   the silence between peals of a temple bell.
22/ They circle, these children, in tunics of red and black; they circle, they
   turn, holding hands, they chant out their rhymes and erratic rhythms,
23/ as a psalm of consolation, with upheld palms— they spiral, these
   barefoot children, they circle, stepping lightly on cast-down palm
   branches
24/ a children's chorus mid-song, releasing a psalm of consolation— it
   unfolds itself as a prayer, a note found in a coat pocket, or years later,
   a scrap paper falling from a forgotten book.
25/ No closing hymns. No descent of saints from the rafters. Not even a
   guilty hallelujah with wounded wings to add a final denouement for
   the scene—
26/ In the end, graffiti covers all stone markers in the abandoned temples and
   churchyards— ten foot tall water-oaks fail and topple— in the end, even
   a child can translate to past memory. We stain our hands with prayers of
   henna, with charcoal— faith smearing across our palms, our mouths.

Venerations of the Temple: Observations of Whitman in Winter 1891

Or, in other words, Walt Whitman as a temple of poetry—
At his window, he sits in winter watching a fractured flock of crows; his right
    hand gesturing in thought—
or absentmindedly stroking his beard,
winter settles around the house. Whitman breathes out sunflowers.
A gift of a kimono rests across his lap, as he rubs a sleeve of silk-patterned-
    magnolias across his face.
Whitman smiling turns the page.
—as he sleeps, hidden in the pale fields of his beard, a clustering of mice,
    blind and hairless, squirm within the tight weavings of their nest
His ink stained fingertips pause over a fresh blank page—
Tonight he dreams of sunflowers— an acre plot of expanding blooms— and
    himself wading in the midst of the tidal pool of gold.
He seals the folded, finished page inside an arcane envelope; drips red wax
    once.
While holding a ripe plum, sweet on the tongue, his epiphany unfolds within
    the act of eating, within the moment shifting; by eating the plum, he eats
    the epiphany, becoming the moment, transposing with the plum—atom
    for atom— the plum becoming a poem, to verse, notions of words on
    the page— so, by eating the plum, he eats the poem, his hunger
    devouring himself in the process to satiate the creative urge—
He devours the world which he contemplates, the world as a deep blood-red
    plum blurring with himself.
Thrumming against the glass, a horsefly crosses the window where Whitman
    sits at his desk.
The pen scratches a phrase—then draws a line through the text
—as a knife in the kitchen slices through a fresh loaf of dark rye bread
—as a carpenter's assistant trudges through late winter snow, arms
    loaded with firewood, scraps of kindling, his red cap bobbing under the
    drawing room windows.
Whitman shifts back in his chair by candlelight as winter descends outside in
    maternal darkness.
The blank page mirrors the lots of snow spreading outside his window.
— cast off by a lantern—hour past sunset, walking within a perimeter of
    arched light—
The fly transposes identities, becoming the poet, the poet becoming the fly.
    A nervous twitch. Divulging of words—broadcasting the basic senses of
    perception—the surface of a plum, or for instance,

By accident the arch of his left hand catches the tail end of a fresh inked
  paragraph, smearing patterns of words, shifting letters into blackbirds—
a small gathering of blue-black shapes against the rime of winter.
Discarded ideas, balls of paper curl into fists of magnolia blooms.
His coat of cedar incense rests over a chair across the room. His hat like a
  patient dog curls in the corner of the bed.
The cap of the carpenter's assistant burns in his mind's eye—persistent
  reminder of lost possibilities.
His denouement shatters, breaks into components of electrons, static
  electricity, the body's song humming along winter tracks, machineries
  celebrated with steaming moment of release, the engines of proportion
  and concord scattering crows of last November into confetti, raucous
  voices of a crowd, elements of a thrumming
  heart, pulsing libido,
Downstairs the housekeeper shuffles plump dough into seven porcelain
  bowls— she covers each vessel under a damp towel.
After sunset, a cluster of lantern lights gather outside his temple windows,
  despite the rain.
—as the young man, still in his red cap, stands in the bedroom doorway,
  waiting, ignored by many; the cluster of visitors watch the old man in
  his sleep—
Whitman becomes the red cap—fabric worn at the edges, frayed slightly.
  He embraces the function, celebrates the moment of the cap atop the
  unkempt head of a blue collar craftsman: the heft of the worker's
  shoulders joining planes of wood, the pulse of hips following the flow of
  a handsaw, the young man humming to himself in pine sawdust—
Sitting on the edge of his bed, the poet's finger marks a closed book. He
  watches winter descend, blurring outside the window.

Saint Brendan and the Nordic Moon

Once again the personal cliché of a crescent moon exists on the horizon—
  but in reality, he remains under cover, Nordic features blurred by his
  unshaven smile as he lies dreaming—
And my son's voice on the child monitor; he calls out in the middle of the
  night, calling from the future, long distance, as if wanting to break
  the miles between—
a cradle moon ripe with summer, leaning heavy over a water-oak branch,
  fracturing the bones of the sentence in mid-phrase, the branch
  snapping in half—
or as a fractured conversation, the cellular lines weak— satellite in nadir orbit,
  breaking sentences in half,
—as Brendan in the backyard dividing his stored collection of stones into two
  piles, his small hands creating moons, granite satellites orbiting his
  slight frame, one by one by—
A wide gray bowl, heavy with ripe peaches, their gold fur glowing against the
  pale ceramic.
—even the moment before the moon becomes snared in tree branches, even
  the second which precedes the net's descent capturing the wild bird,
  before the thrumming of wings, the rapid staccato language beating
  the air, rhythmic repetition.
As a starting point: the cradle crescent. The boy. The bridge with barn
  swallows building their mud nests. Clusters of new moons joined as a
  hive, endless flights arcing across and under the other— in the back
  seat, the boy asleep unaware of his world shifting around him, as the
  afternoon shifts forward, its moon lowering over the bridge one
  more time.
The poem itself splintering into shards, falling apart into a flock of swallows,
  a pattern within a pattern; Saint Brendan as a child, witnessing the
  fraction of the whole flock, scattering in cycles surrounding him and
  the mathematics of dreaming.
The full weight of the evening does not affect the migratory patterns of
  meandering barn swallows as they fall Southeast to the forgotten
  Missionary of the Moon— a ruined cathedral of ghost limestone built by
  Saint Brendan in an obscure century, off the eastern coastline of
  North America— now covered in bramble, bird scat, decades of
  swallow nestings, and eggshell fragments, the small squat church
  leaning under the abundant burden of the sky—

The bite of a blunt knife, trimming back the fur of a wild peach.

After the major storm moved out of the Gulf, heading northward, all the fruit
        trees went into hurricane-shock, the branches standing bare on one
        side, the other half— erupting into blossoms— out of season.

Another reality: north of the Crescent City, a boy barely eighteen lies choking
        with life, the restrictions on his body taking control— only the
        passing moon pauses in his wandering arc to lift the boy out of his
        final epiphany, and carry him to the edge of the skyline—

In his new hagiography, Brendan as a child sits in the backyard sketching
        crescent ideograms in wet sand, building islands out of river pebbles.
        Shadows of swallows pass across his face, bridging the distance
        between himself and a sudden epiphany.

The rough pit of a peach under the heavy stumbling tongue.

Memories of the first landing, the first island: disembarking from the weather-
        beaten bark, stepping onto blonde, wet sand— the trade winds heavy
        as a new life pressing on the Saint's back—

As leaning into a new language, new cartography sketched on the palm of a
        nervous hand— you map the night sky with the middle finger's tip
        aligned to the North Star, your back against the past, against the
        homeward path—

—and then the first bite of the first found peach growing wild in the obscure
        New World— here is where Saint Brendan founded his church,
        beside a displaced fruit tree, on an island lost to maps, forgotten by
        history.

A small gnarled tree of the New World with a boat crescent lowering off the
        bottom branches; as a returning, an imminent departure back home,
        moving back from foreign soil.

—in the end, make my form into the wandering moon which follows beside
        your highway. As he stammers haltering psalms in your ears. A
        persistent icon sidetracked in his orbit of decay. Remember, son, in
        all aspects of this fragmented world— I will never leave you.

Saint Brendan and the Whale

Hunched over and divine, the humpback whale dives into immeasurable
fathoms of text, into handwritten gospel, dispensing metric counts of
syllables within clouds of plankton or microscopic manna, lingering
fogs of marine krill and left over scum of wandering monkfish—all
the while motioning beyond the Known, the Seen.

White-haired, ruddy-cheeked— even in his dreams Brendan gains the burning
sensation of salt on skin, salt as a deity's essence rubbing up against
his humanity. The sea transforming the saint to manuscript, to sacred
writ, planing down all that is mortal, reducing his form into codex, to
bound papyrus. Erasure of the mortal frame into an illuminated
scroll—arabesque calligraphy converting the body to holy text.

Call him Leviathan. Behemoth. Ishmael. But do not limit him to these
syllables or to the formula of these letters.

On his small drifting boat, as he sleeps, the saint builds bridges, creates
hyperboles between calfskin and blubber. He sketches rough maps in
charcoal on vellum scraps, narrow strips of leather—detailed records
of steps across green-gray water.

Resurfacing, the whale shifts form to a creature of pebble and barnacle, echo
and canyon—

The tongue burns the hand with scripture.

The Atlantic Ocean is to a book of gospels as a male humpback whale is to a
cathedral: hallowed and sacred.

On the edge of the horizon his boat leans—a filament of meat caught
between the teeth, between silence and the opening chant of morning
mass, between burning match and exposed thumb—

For there are times when a whale is not a whale but an island.

The boat leans as a suggestive call from a street corner, syllables vibrate
slightly upon release, rhythms tremble in the night air.

The entire being of a baleen whale becomes the essence of his song, the
   filtering of memory into a personal response, an echoing chant into
   the fathoms of water which call out for recognition, or prompt an
   obscene overture, graceless and churlish—

Sometimes a saint does not define himself as a saint.

The notion of the baroque tenses within the mating call of a male humpback
   whale; his open desires reverberate thousands of miles underwater,
   his declarations translate to ambient scriptures, the slow drift of
   continents, the drag of glaciers.

He becomes as a Latin phrase scrawled in pencil along the margin of a used
   book, the script mirroring waves, the curve of a tail-fin in apogee, or
   a hand gesturing. In return, the saint dreams himself leaning within
   his scriptorium, face lost in the depths of holy seas. He hunches close
   to the ebb and flow of fresh-inked scriptures, blue waves lapping
   against his coarse clerical robes. His shadow unfolds against the stone
   library walls, a blue-finned rorqual, breaching forward, then
   submerging into the tidal night.

Saint Brendan among Autumn Cypress

i. temple
Jazz this dark
   collects under the skin:
a spreading bruise of twilight
   pooling as rainwater within
a grappling knot
   of cypress trees in autumn—
      blood-rust shining through every leaf.
   He stands, the saint, un-gathered
in prayer, interlaced with phrasings of devout
   petition, supplication, hands opened—
          •

It was once possible to sketch
   the atlas of the known world
across a saint's calloused palm,
   the right hand trembling, burdened
 with the weight of Western Europe
   and cumbersome hints of the North African coastline—
      as a suggested offering of bundled
   spices, scrimshaw carvings of whales.
In the manner a saint's luminosity
   echoes an Irish ground beetle
Nebria brevicollis, metallic blue-black
   in blue twilight, the insect foraging under
cypress roots in continual pursuit, seeking
   closure, as a law unto itself, burrowing
in dark earth, leaving dirt under the nails,
   in the lifelines of the palm.
      This was his first temple.
     Living wood arched. Buckled.
Each cardinal point of the compass
   assigned a representative. In an open embrace.

ii. boat
Was there a time, when caught
   in the lap and lull and foam and lurch
of the north driven current,

did he look down at the worn leather
of his sandals, the frayed bottom hem and
     loose threads of his faded robe?
          Did he feel the jazz of his moment open out
     to surround him in a strange monstrous doubt,
in a burgeoning lack of purpose as he drifted,
     cowled in his cypress planked boat?

iii. coffin
Sometimes *boat* translates to *coffin*,
     unexpectedly, without an epiphany
to balance out the motions of acceptance
     or denial— yourself drifting forward
patiently: without oars, without
     sails, following the random current,
          the gold-green thread leading you through
     the full labyrinth, the circular snarled knot of
triskelion waves, circles
     within circles within—
In the past you laid out
     cypress planks, joining each without allowance
for error or gap between the slabs of timber,
     the cross spine gathered into a hull,
a keel, a developing outer shell,
     watertight with overlapping boards
          held with rosehead nails, piercing wood
     in roves or preferred tree nail pegs
gripping the planks coated with a layer of tar
     and goat hair, sealing the impervious box.
This small temple still exists as a letter to the future, preserved
     and bundled— the body as paper, stained with the holy testament
across the creases and folds of flesh before burial,
     every word recorded— the linen shroud of your moment discolored
with Latin inscriptions, scrolls of text wrapped

in phrases broken off into a refrain, words of prayer circles—
    Asperges me hysopo, et mundabor:
  lavabis me, et super nivem dealbabor.
Auditui meo dabis gaudium et laetitiam:
  et exsultabunt ossa humiliata.
       •

So it lies, your last shrine— remaining
  a testament to an awkward faith
of a saint interred within a cypress—
    the full tempo of your moment: *diminuendo,*
passionato, hanging hesitantly, a delicate pause
    between. As a figure lost between continents,
        in a continual drift
  of slow precision, with insistence.
A metaphor within itself, with twilight
  merging over a line of cypress trees.

An Untitled Poem for Beth

Did this time ever really exist?

I mean this scene, of you
and I in a small, dive bar,
lost alongside the river front, where the ghosts
of the past wander among the living,
not as I once thought, out of loneliness,
but as a means of remembering themselves.

Only I seem able to see them tonight,
lost in the renovations, the reconstructions founded
to house local bands, joints patronized by women
with too bright make-up, neon lips, dark eye shadow,
and men who tie their unwashed hair back in a long,
slender tail.

Honestly I am trying to avoid the past,
as much as I am trying to avoid this present, ignore
the eyes of the dead, as they casually touch
a shoulder, kiss an upturned face.
Unseen, they stroke us, watch the patterns
we dance on the wooden floors. They watch me,

as I try relating to the irony of you dancing with me, two friends
with a music heavy in bass, electric sequences,
and an off tempo drummer.
                    I feel out of place,
almost a ghost myself trying to pass as someone else,
a ghost of a fox perhaps, wearing the awkward guise

of human form, the disguise of a receding hairline, lanky arms,
a red-pine beard.
You're here to recover from a relationship.
Or to become the person you never were, as a character
in a German film, someone named Marion, dancing in European pubs,
searching for something she knows doesn't exist.

In Somer, I have you say,
denk ich am liebsten.
Or maybe you should speak *de dialogos espanoles,*
pequenas revueltas, como la noche
veia tus expresiones
mientras haciamos el amor–

I suppose now I've created a displacement
with you and the verse, the same displacement I felt
during my college years, the same scenes I play back
as I try to drift into sleep, a self-induced sadism, a wanting
to change patterns of past events, the confusions,
the fumblings with sexuality. And see,

I've transformed these sentences,
so they no longer resemble a quilt,
or an embellished collage. They've become nothing
but a collection of ramblings,
broken metaphors,
myself trying too hard

to be Frank O'Hara
lost in another city.
Once, I've even tried to raise his shade,
to allow his light into my darkening rooms,
to apologize,
to idolize–

But now, let me step back,
find my place in this new moment,
of writing for you a poem of discovery,
of finding yourself wandering among emotions,
over confessionals in phone booths,
of flash and dagger nights,

with white wine and Hoosier bars,
dancing with a poet who has given up on love
for the love of words, of images.
Years from now, do not forget the living
you have accomplished, the varieties of self gained—
Let these nights remain with you,

locked in eternal recollection,
the ghost of your youth linked
arm-in-arm with your present tense,
waltzing softly forward, with half steps,
inching ever closer to the ever present future,
his form lingering, waiting just on the edge of the horizon.

Section 2: Fragments of a Self Portrait

This thought is as a death, which cannot choose
But weep to have that which it fears to lose.
    —William Shakespeare
    'Sonnet #64"

On his way home, he may be watching this—the moon at daybreak after
  I waited throughout the night
    —Fujiwara No Teika
    trans. Hiroaki Sato and Burton Watson

i.

The mirror reflects a dense image of myself
in the mornings and evenings, when the halflight
pours out into the room, an open vase
spilling image, shadow. When I turn to face

my face, this is when I lose recognition
of the man you once knew; transformation
into a winged egret, silent metamorphosis,
grey-tipped feathers turning in excess, spiraling out towards—

This is the hour Caravaggio
worked, the time of modeling, of *imitatio*,
transference of a boy's flesh from urchin
to saint, dirt still under the nails, the skin
glowing with street life, with pale mirroring
of the city to canvas, to paint, echoing

ii.

Recently, I dreamt about your hands, cold
against my own, stressing the differences
we always felt, but never acknowledged, until—

and strange, after four years, your image still holds
my memory tight, reshapes my words—that since
your leaving—still lie along the mind's edge.

You were beautiful to me. Once. Certain
as the sounds of approaching rain,
the dampness in the distance, yet inherent,
undeniable, as motions through trees, spent

emotions we collected.   Do I lie, tell you
I discovered someone else, someone new?
Do I tell you his beauty is like a fine, dense rain,
as a flood of levees, drowning out the horizon line—

—towards the waning moon, visible even
now at this hour of the morning, a paleness
repeating my freckled nature—and your hands
white as winter sunrise, fragile, a dangerous
flirting with strangers, moving always
to replace me with another—

  One summer, for politics, I shaved
my head down to nothing, to a brief blue burr,
transforming my face to a wartime criminal,
pink triangles sewn on my clothing, my coats.

Death grinned, accented his soft bones;
the skeleton exposed in my facial features
left me, not as a plump Caravaggio boy,
but as the painter Schiele, withdrawn, the language cloyed

iv.

—against the words that a friend speaks, her mouth
moving with news of you and how you changed.

There are days when all I remember is your moth-like
anger, the movement into fury, emotions arranged,
flitting before lanterns, house lights flickering
with you drunk on emotion, on vodka or gin,
the eyes darkening, a tide rising quicker than
your hands.   And honestly, there is no one new since

last March. My lovers only exist as
brief imaginings, or brief fondling in a car—
their eyes the color of azurite, exhausted
with tremors of pale wanting, the color
of early morning, the hour of my waiting, when I
used to wait for your return, pretending not to be waiting.

v.

She always laughs as Diana, hiding herself
under folds of cotton, the pulsing plush
circling, circling with the nature
of aviaries, the spirits of language pushed
to the front of her mouth   How the taste of apples,
small and tart, mimics the taste of a tongue darting
between a couple kissing in dark alleys,
emotions exchanged, after hours, the night hardening
against them as they lean into each other.

The manner I wanted to exist: without
question, undeniable. No one ever
understood this thirst, this want to drink deeper
the essence, a mutual possession flowing.
An electric current. The arc of pulsing wings.

vi.

This is the hour Phil reads his art aloud—
the language, each word, with tiny wings lifting,
circling off his tongue— the words spiral out,
rare birds arching into the room, shifting
into aviary, into verbiage
all its own; even Phil's form shudders into
bird or angel. As a dark-water crane he emerges,
a metamorphosis, a change for the new
gesture of the text— startled these starlings flock
awake, this hour, the same hour as before,
but bluer, more intense. It deepens with the fluid clock,
with Phil's voice motioning into the room, a score
of syllables, a tide pulling back with images: the ear becomes
a door opening to a stranger, his coat rich with plumages.

vii.

Even here, with the fluid pulse of the body
drowning in the shower, I think of you
and the one who came after, replacing the library
of my body, replaced movement of my hands through
your hair, almost shoulder length, my hands core
of inspiration, acts of clichéd expression,
which you took as mockery.
                                        I reclaim these sores
in my hands, paper cuts in soft skin, the one
pale scar on my right thumb, across the root
of the palm, the crescent cuticles worn,
the callused flesh which gently cupped your blunt
self, stroked the smoothness of your storming
ego. My rough hands now only hold abstractions
of myself: the vacuums of remaining subtractions.

viii.

—a cup of coffee for instance, or a postcard
of Frank O'Hara, nineteen fifty, his arms crossed,
poised, the eyes intent for the moment the shutter
clicks closed. His lips open partly to speak a word,
a phrase.   But this time is past, the word lost,

just as the years we spent arguing with bitter
accusations over misplacement of glasses,
or newspapers scattered across the bedroom,
or changing the cat's litter box, domestic
wrestlings of dependency.   Even the radio's jazz
recalls the anger in your tongue, your drunken loom—
miscalculated distance of footfall and the sickly
green colored floor of the Saint Louis flat;
the images transform to nightmares, more than that, they

ix.

—emerge from under trees. And you appear
shirtless, male warmth breathing in the cool morning air,
breathing out steam, a Spanish horse pacing
                              or maybe,
instead, an eagle circling tight spirals, a pause
in motion, blind language merging. Moving from under
the trees, your form drowns me, without you aware
of the swollen river in my blood, torrential
rains filling me, an empty vase—
                              but then suppose
the warm hands which hold me now are yours, instead of
being my own, washing out memories of you,
rinsing the body's text and past references,
impressions remaining from fingertips once pressed,
slipping along my lower spine, causing sensations as blue
as the night you first called me *lover.*   The moment still drenches

—but no, wait, what I need to say remains hidden
somehow under words, under language of ravens,
or the memories of your touch, rare and sudden,
without warning, as I drift into sleep. It lends
itself to catalogs, the listing of actions
for the hands, fingers caressing, clasping themselves
        or the heft of apples, situations
between two men wrestling in orchards, grasping
the lift and sway of the other's limbs
close to motions of the other, after
the day's work, the harvesting from tree limbs

And you really always kept your hair short, tattered
as Roman Caesar or Brando as Brutus, shorn
close to the skull, almost as a figure in mourning, or

xi. Listen, Close:
(Magnolia grandiflora)

for Lowell

Listen, close. You can hear the pale subtle
opening of the magnolia blossoms
willing out their voices in St. Louis.
Euclid Avenue darkens with their heavy,
lifting mouths, their burning with memory,
low murmurs of your voice absent now from cafés—

And there was a time I meant to tell you more,
how you unfurled in me aspects I once thought
were lost, portions that made up my whole
voice— as a whisper in Spanish: *nadamos*
en los ojos de dios or *tus manos*
language made liquid to echo the flow
of your warm gestures, your fluid words.   *Listen*,
as memories of you fall from my pen.

xii.

I cannot justify my wanting you
still, even to myself, even on days
like this, when I wander, lost in a haze
of past lives.   Was it nineteen o' two
or in nineteen twenty when we first met
seven years before my grandmother's birth?

Under remote bridges you hesitantly let
me kiss you, a calculated risk worth
chancing among the needles, used condoms

but no, that was nineteen ninety two, after
your marriage failed, justification then
for my holding you deep in Creve Coeur Park, a secret
folding, intricate, within itself, as between two men,
not as the opening of a pure passion,
but a spiraling inward. An unresolved question.

xiii. You in Darkness

I am tired of writing of windows. Tired
of describing how the light falls between us, making
your touch seem the caress of a fallen angel, wings
Spread above me, a tent of suffocating light.
I want to describe you in darkness, in the hours
before sleep. I want to describe you with your right hand
Pressing the small of my back or the nape of my neck,
your voice whispering fragments.
The darkness will be a heavy tide, drowning
The church clock, silencing the chimes that circumvent
our lives. The pulse of night will follow our motions,
the rhythms of your hips over mine.
                                        Set by the window,
the sides of a filled vase bead water, just as
small drops of humidity cling to your quieting face.

xiv.

2:30 in the morning and down the hallway
the neighbors are fighting, worse than any of our
arguments. Sounds filter through the thin walls,
circle above and around my room. Their words sway,
spiral the ceiling fan's blades, until the half hour,
when numb and half asleep some predatory phrase recalls
a time when you fisted the air, almost against—

Then he slaps her— or worse— her muffled wails
rise. Fall again. The police eventually appear

a manner which drowns me, if one can be
swallowed in another's image, another's fear,
or the instant a contact occurs with the failing
beauty of another's history, or a drunken fist
raised against the retelling of a personal story

Some mornings, after an hour's run, after a slight
shower, I reconsider my body, still damp with steam
in the bathroom mirror, glowing with a persistent light.
The skin gains a halo, a quality that almost seems
religious, as a self-portrait by Schiele, reds and greens
accenting the lines of the form, a figure framed in self
reflection, in the blur of early hours, when time
becomes an old man fumbling with his money belt,
with his pockets, he clowns around as if he has quarters, dimes
to pick among as he stands in doors of buses, bellowing
about his poor health, his age, bad eyes. Help him
move along, forward into the evening—
                                        even now,
without full closure, he shifts from under the leaves
of evening, light motioning from mirrors, the hour easing—

xvi.

When he first moves towards you, covers himself
with your body— does the moment ever surpass
the time you came in my arms, shivering,
mouth slack, my legs tangled round your slender
frame   When he shifts and holds your arched spine, a wealth
in his rough hands, do your eyes tremble, as glass
in midsummer storms, do your limbs quiver
with his tongue touching the seven moles wintering
in the fleece of your sex, the down between your legs, plush

    With me, your body always opened as a book
or an unfolding of crows, all of a sudden,
without warning, feathers lifted, pushed
upwards and out, dark plumes merged, the sweaty inner skin broke
free, until we lay in our damp bodies, all sodden and

—or the photos Mike & Tommie & I found
of a woman spreading open her legs
before a man's eager mouth. I was ten
at the time and still don't understand
the insistence the others felt bound
to watch: a series unfolding, the tugs
of flesh between male and female, the bends
of positioning, intricate knots, bland
greed expressed on boys' faces
                as figures
of myth, Herakles holding the heavens
temporarily on his back with seven stars
of early morning entangled in his dark hair,
his shaking arms heavy, pinned up against the arc
of closed sky— a moment of exhilaration

xviii.

—the times I slept alone. Dreaming my slack
body over you, your winged shoulders spread, your back
carried the weight of my body
                    the heavy weight
of the horizon. My trembling hands translated
your form into a winged Assyrian bull,
a support of my desire   as a figure
of myth, circling   a broken recording,
Beethoven's sonata number fourteen,
opus twenty-seven in an endless loop, coursing
through the blood, in the head, repetitious, a lean
fragmentation of a longer body of work,
unlimited chorus, lush, a starling lung-ing
into the night with its song, transporting
its desire beyond impulse, the voice plunging

—the moment singer and song become one, as a poster
of an artist on stage, eyes clenched in a concentration,
body half exposed, body thrown in lyrics, fostering
emotions expressed with the mike clenched close to the motions
of want, as a bird translates the song it sings nightly,
or the poet who becomes the language flighting across
the moon's halo, moth-like, wings spread slightly,
arched in the moment the painter transcends her painting, a cross
between being and seeming.
        As two mouths meet, words exchanged—
as Orpheus torn apart mid-song, mid-phrase, sentences
broken, leaving nouns spilling forth, verbs jutting, disarranged,
internal phrasings dangling; his beautiful wrenches
of despair bloodied with adjectives. His admirers,
still maddened, hold portions of the whole, the splintered mirror

xx.

A passing car radio blares *Saint Louis*
woman with her diamond ring— Saint Louis woman—
Bessie Smith's voice disappears beyond the brewery,
beyond Farmer's Market and obscure streets
lingering in south Soulard, locations which sum
the parts of our relationship, the beats

of our rhythms just off center to each other.
But even fragments of her blues are still cutting,
fracture portions of self to the despair
flung out from her body, from her throat, notes trilling
against the arch of open sky exhilarating
the moment, challenged between earth and sky, waiting
for release, an opening
                              like myself, still wanting to wake,
to find beside me the quiet glances of your warm face

Section 3: To A Former Lover in Minneapolis

Take a phrase, then
fracture it—

—Lynda Hull
"Ornithology

Elegy for Gary: January 10, 1994

The world seems heavy with your sudden absence,
  gravity more persistent. I feel the weight
      of your leaving, a heavy shifting in my mattress,
an emptiness pushed into my arms,

as dense as the new moon's form, dirt lingering
  on his arms, his thighs. He has just planted the new year
      in place, the leaf-green months spreading out, mingling
with the air, a forest of new growth—

each lip-shaped leaf represents a different day,
  each branch a different week, twining forward,
      opening in time. The moon leans, clips away
a shaft of past growth, the strand for your time,

the short week and few days your existence
  was spent, fighting to breathe in this new year.
      The moon bends the branch circular, into a wreath to wear.
The tenth day shines darkly in his bright hair.

Metamorphosis

The moon was not even aware of him,
of the boy climbing the water tower,
  a figure held against the graffiti
      and a rising tempo of the moment.

The boy was suspended above time. Above
the town. And though the moon did not watch him,
  he watched the moon. The slow rowing across
      still water. At the top of the tower

he paused, opened his arms as if to take
in the silent crescent on the horizon,
  or even the town itself, as if one
      could embrace rejection. In a sense

he became the moon, a paleness spreading
his arms— or rather, he opened them
  as a memory, as my memory,
      of the time I was seventeen and knew

I was different, but could not name it;
only felt the presence here, in my chest,
  a rhythm beating at night, as I tried
      to conform my thoughts to what I was told,

what I was taught. The drumming never ceased.
It grew, over the months and years, became
  a persistent hum in my ears, my throat
      breathing with the motion, until I saw

myself for what I was: a pale changeling,
my form metamorphosed to a bird,
  soft feathers covered my hands and shoulders,
      a soft down of my new self surrounding

my form like a warm coat, a strong embrace
of acceptance; the kind I wish for this boy,
   for this scene of the boy alone. He breathes
      in the moment: his blue hour tightens.

He arches his back and falls forward,
into the arms of emptiness, of night.
   Can you imagine such a falling?
      The denial of the self arching the body,
casting it into a death of scandals.
I used to stand on rooftops, on houses
   to feel the moment of it all, to try
      and abandon myself into the wind.

But I realize now, I am like Horace,
an old man chasing young girls and servants,
   all for the sensations of past flights
      of fancy, a man picturing himself

with wings, a singing bird tonguing the moon
with songs of beauty in a passing face,
   the hard-hearted boys that tempted him
      with their hard bodies, their rough sports.

My wings cannot take me backwards in time,
to change events swallowed by history.
   I hover softly in the present times,
      cursing my lack of angelic powers,

wanting to will myself to the falling,
hold back the events. Cast the boy's form
   into a new image, into the shape of a passing swallow,
      or a young swan shifting eastward—by night.

Herakles Wrestling With Death

At first I was not surprised by the coldness
of his flesh when we embraced, our arms locking together,
his fingers nestling under my elbow,
caressing the back of my neck.
  The shock came later,
when I realized his body hollow, made up
of only sinew and muscle, the way Botticelli
painted his Venus, her body without bones, crossing
the horizon in an endless free-fall
around the Earth, bobbing below God's eyes
as an angelic satellite, or weather balloon.

This is the way she appeared in my dreams at sixteen,
her arms opening towards me.
We'd dance slow spirals until I'd wake
in a damp bed, my grandmother outside
spreading sheets to dry in the morning air,
the whole wash moving in a white tide, fluttering
in a cold circle around her,

as close as Death clinging tightly to me,
his body heavy with cholera, his crew-cut scraping
my cheek and neck as we struggled to throw
the other, until his lips brushed up against mine,
cold.
  As if by accident, his free arm slipped
between my legs and paused a second too long, allowing
the contest to become something
other.
  We fell then,
together, the heavy crows caged inside him
flurrying wildly.
                    •
In my old neighborhood, crows would cluster
in the pine trees like immigrants from distant countries.

Boys with air rifles would aim wildly
at their sudden movements, at the blurs of charcoal
flashing from tree top to tree top.

Even grown men would attempt these targets,
drunk with lack of responsibilities and dollar drafts,
they wanted the dark bodies to plunge down at their feet,
a bundle of feathers and bones,
the same way my brother died,
huddled on a stranger's lawn, the shiftings
in his chest erratic. The August air humid in his lungs.

•

Now, in another neighborhood,
further north of my past, you and I walk
in the beginnings of winter, occasionally letting the arms
of our coats brush together.

At the highway overpass, surrounded
by Asian graffiti and eyes of billboards,
we pause between columns, soak in each other's restlessness.

Your face shifts with the motions of my fingertips,
with the steady hum of late night commuters overhead.

Flickering between expressions, we become
each other's death; me, wanting to take off
the rings on your married hands. And you
in the shadows, holding my brother's youth
in your sienna eyes.

Metamorphosis: Ode to Kenny Fries

I want to hold you
  in my camera, preserve the quiet nature
    of this scene, of you sleeping, the bed sheets
pulled up from around you, wings opening,
  yourself lying as Hesphestus resting,
    muscles still taut from smithing new armors.
      When I tried holding you that summer,
  you spilled from my hands, a fountain,
an overflowing of words; you could not even
  fit in my mouth, your language filling me
entire, choking me with poetry,
      with masculinity as I read verses aloud,

your voice slipping from my lips,
  possessing my tongue with your texts.
    When we kissed, a slight taste
of salt lingered, the ocean intent on staying,
  remaining with us, even at nightfall
    with the soft lowering of your clothes,
      a lowering of the tides. This is the same day
  your landlord tore out of the earth the old oak in the backyard;
noise from the saws ran along the cape all afternoon, into the night,
  ripping across the white beach houses, the narrow streets,
reaching the men in the dance bars dancing slowly in pairs.
      Your body remained heavy with the afternoon.

I still remember your sweet weight over me,
  sand lingering secretly on your skin, in your scalp.
    And with the morning sun, the sheets spread out,
from your upper spine, exposed portions of your body to me,
  exposed the back that supported my love-making.
    A horse neighed in the distance.
      The sun blazed up higher,
  exposing you as the god of metal-work,
the god that broke my name under his hammer
  creating myths out of smith, the god with bird-like bones,
a god I cannot encompass,
      with my human hands.

Herakles Crossing the River

1.

At first there is no arrival— rather,
there is nothing to show that you have arrived,
until you adjust to the low lighting,

to the strange grass growing about you,
and the cries of strange birds flying overhead.
But I should start further back,

begin this recital with a different collection
of words. Begin with the river that runs
through my childhood, where my father plants bulbs

of amaryllis, dragon's breath. By spring
small green tongues appear, murmuring
a soft language, telling stories

of happenings below the earth,
how the dead wait to be ferried across
a river of smoke, their voices

thick with various accents, their arms heavy
from carrying bundles of memories and trunks of photographs.
Such stories my father would tell me before

my afternoon naps; I would dream of his ghosts appearing translucent
as paper lanterns or will-o'-wisps, lights darting in the distance,
just as the fireflies burned across the river I tried to swim across,

but always failed, losing breath,
and in the end merely floated a dead man's float,
the water reflecting back stars

as I waited for my muscles to stop shaking,
for the trembling to leave my arms,
so I could begin the slow lap home.

2.
In my arms, you tremble like the new moon, traveling
across the horizon, a body shaking from rowing all night
across the thickness of the black waters of forgetfulness.

Even your hands quiver slightly
in the middle of an embrace, your small bones
under mine, your slender body almost

like a woman's. Or, as a fresh shoot of sunflower seedlings,
planted by my father, a field of them shivering in the early morning,
the horizon consumed with their open, yellow mouths.

This sight was always a satisfaction for my father,
the field relieving him for a moment
from the duty of care.

Allowing him the satisfaction of a release,
like pulling back layers of flesh from a pomegranate
or pulling language from the throat,

the moment when the word and the speaker are one,
the way a hummingbird and an amaryllis are united,
a second when bird and flower are consumed

in a blur of motion. Like the motions of your hands,
hovering over my heart,
my eyes.

3.
Before crossing the river,
the priests shaved off my body hair,
anointed me with oils, placed a coin

in my mouth, a strand of frankincense
around my neck. They draped me with a sheet
of muslin cloth and I began my descent.

There are days when all I remember
is the gloom of the Afterlife, the restlessness
of the dead. How they gamble parts of their bodies,

some winning extra femurs, extra ribs to decorate
their spines. Some wander empty-armed, a hazy
whisper in the vision of my memory,

the way the white peacocks wandered
in the dark gardens of Hell, among the pools
and fountains reflecting pale nothing.

And then sometimes, there is a comfort
from the kiss of a friend, bringing back
the rough face of my father, talking me into sleep,

the humidity collecting in the room,
my father's face moon-like over the bed's horizon,
and behind him, small yellow stars,

the field of sunflowers rising
and falling in afternoon tides of his voice
and the muslin curtains lifting around me.

Metamorphosis: Odè to an Olympic Diver

There are times when you appear, without warning,
   deus ex machina, your figure as an angel
      walking along the arches of heaven
before the dive, the moment
   of hesitation, a precise time
      before translation, before your actions
         of folded arms and legs, and wings
   emerge from angles of bone and flesh—
change into origami papers: Japanese cranes
   leaping out towards the moon—
or pale marsh egrets flashing their wings in wide arcs
   open to the night sky—
but I am not a sculptor, I am a poet.
   My body was fashioned to stand motionless,
      withdrawn, a gray-brown fedora on my head,
cloaked in a long, winter coat. Only
   my hands were made to move,
      puppets, marionettes dancing across paper,
         accenting phrases when I talk aloud,
   even to myself, or in my sleep, my fingers tapping,
knotting themselves in nervous positions.
   Even at this moment, trying to motion myself
into this verse, my hands become agitated with me,
      angry that their only function
is to raise an apple to my lips, serve as figures
   of transportation from plate
      to mouth. They want more out of life,
to create words flowing, a new text,
   or to recreate your figure in clay,
      knead life into the earth, raise
         a motion into your elevated limbs,
   a figure in motion, animated life poised above me.
Sometimes, posing before mirrors, I stand naked,
   worry about the pale conditions of my body:
it will never know you, but then, in the gymnasiums,

I push to transform my image,
to move towards a higher function,
  to be more than just a word-smith,
    breathing words into the ears of the public,
syllables across the eyes of librarians. Do you hesitate
  before the fall? Do you dream as a bird?
      I've been told when a young swift travels across western Europe,
      it motions through instinct only, never landing, never ceasing to be
anything other than a mere vehicle of flight, of wings.
It feeds on insects in the air, sleeps in higher altitudes on drafts,
  currents of high winds. It knows not how to fall.
I once wondered of these motions,
      of the insistence of gravity's pull back to earth,
or my persistent nightmares of my father, scenes with his doppelganger
  dropping my brother into a well, or a bottomless cavern.
      Dark, unbidden thoughts of children.
If I try, I recreate the fear inside my chest;
  the same fear when I took the first fall
      into deeper Gulf waters, learning to swim, my father behind me,
        invisible to the trauma. His insistence
to submerge me I could not understand—but my brother,
I kept trying to make him grow wings, against his falling,
  to raise him back into waiting arms,
return him back to the folding of security, into a warmth,
  body no longer held by water, but by parental strengths.
Swimming for me now is different.
 There no longer exists a curiosity
      of the loss in gravity. Swimming now
is effortless in a sense, merely a means to be alone,
  floating, almost motionless. The old fears,
      and the memories, return at this time,
again unbidden, but as an adult I've learned
  to shut them off. Close the eyes tighter and
cast them away as stones, into the bottom
  of the tides. I remain, as yourself, poised above,
hands reaching out for something unseen, as a stolen Greek statue,
  glorious and defiant in fragmentation.

Herakles Burning the Pyre

The fire that on my bosom preys
Is lone as some volcanic isle;
No torch is kindled at its blaze—
A funeral pyre.
                    —Lord Byron

Tonight, unable to sleep,
my dreams are invaded continuously
with large mouths of a flowering amaryllis, and memories
of Hylas' red hair, the slow burning
of his motions. Even the slightest gesture
from his body brought a heat of desire
to my thoughts, a cloak of fire to wear—
as when I was younger and fell into
piles of burning leaves, rubbish pyres

brought together by my father.
I do not remember the pain anymore,
only the panic of being covered,
finding myself swallowed in a blurring
of blue tipped heat, the fear becoming
a heavy coat.
            Later, recovery
was only a matter of short waiting:
only, as if the skin grafts were a slight
offering to the pain, my back

an altar, a small testament of future trials.
Afterwards, eight or nine
scars remained, ridges Hylas fingertipped
as if reading braille, reading the text
of my body, as I read his, smoothing
out a translation of wanting between
ourselves. But desire only remains
as long as one feeds it new books, new boys,
ideas to keep the small dragon happy.

It's difficult relating this,
sometimes. The years covering me are vague;
translucent events have occurred, frequent
as lovers who have appeared in my bed,
as plenty as wives I've kept, collections
of children sired... yet, the mere reflection
of a horizon line burning at dusk
brings back the motions he and I gathered,
the subtle wrestlings between us,
the sensations of burning brush
that stemmed from his hands, his breath— surrounding
me in a presence of marshes in flames,
as the swamps of my childhood being cleared
by farmers wanting more territories.
•

In the end, I should have seen the changes,
his casual tones, misplacement of time.
Even now, remembering, my throat feels
constricted, the dark loss smothers

me back to the day when I found
Hylas asleep, covered partly by arms
of a dark haired girl. His bright face displayed
a drowning, consumption in desire
of another. Like my scarred face, swallowed
in memory, moved by images
of a boy, the youth I once was—
but for now—watch as I put on this thin blood shirt,
this bloody desire. I will sacrifice

my past and become a column,
a pillar of anger, of flames, full consumption of memory.
I will fall back into the arms of my father
as he takes me into his bright house,
into the many rooms of his menagerie of warm constellations.
In the end, I will become a motion cross the night skies.
Transforming to a forewarning of fractured possibilities.
An eternal burning of insatiable want.

Still Life with Cardoon and Parsnips
After a painting by Juan Sánchez Cotán (circa 1602)

1.
—as an effort to steal away the breath
circling warm inside your mouth, lingering
with the taste of green onions, pale currants,
something other than burnt coffee and tobacco:

those sweet addictions which filled out your days and hours.
Despite the past histories, the failings between,
there was a time I would step into your arms, into
the dark embrace. You: my addiction, my unrest.

Nights I try writing you down. Fingering
uprooted bulbs, memories stifled with a want
to replace— but let's move forward, ignore the flow
of confessions of broken desire, ignore

the lost love, establish the new scene as a still life:
a table gathered in shadows, burdened with fruits,

2.
Depths of burnt sienna. Raw umber.
The colors of your eyes when dusk settled
over the horizon. The idea of you
always coming over me as a fierce Apollo,

a false sun god rising to flay the words
held in my mouth, the piping rhythm slumbering
on my tongue.   Your bruising love unsettled
portions of my identity, the rise and sway,

the change of inner politics, a slow
erasure of what I motioned towards.
Almost as a consumption of the whole, this love
left me in corners of theaters, in shadows,

or coarse boxes with lifted lids, an exposed, partial view
of unseen contents. Leaving me still wanting to hold you,

3.
of the day, when you told me—
when the light struck cross your face, cross your body
framed in the doorframe: a distant, immobile
Apollo, haloed in afternoon, ruddy

and golden, with lips even then I wanted to claim,
motion against my mouth, with words slipping
iced. Deconstructed.
       Bundled roots left unclaimed
in disappearing light, the motions ripping

across or fragmenting my ideals of what you
and I called love, if ever such a thing
existed between us. What remains are a few
moments I do not spend lost surging

in memories of your denial, pale as white
titanium. Blinded with shades of yellow ochre light.

4.
—with a greening cardoon, the herb rising curved,
arched, leaning back, almost circular.
The fibrous stalk touches past and present
in the same instant, just as two motions are spent

between lovers, removal of clothing
from the edge of each other's lingering stillness,
searching among layers for hidden skin,
the pits of peaches, or two cold plums, sins

associated with meetings of flesh
to flesh, handfuls of you spilling forth—   Men are like fish
when roused, motioning back, as salmon arching
in rapids, darting from present to past, lurching

forward as though drunk, blood slumbering in the veins
waiting to be called,
                    motioned forward into remains

To a Former Lover in Minneapolis

1.
Without provocation,
from the swells
of the unmade bed,

my subconscious pulls you into view
encased in a raw youthfulness.
Once again, you rise in my dreams:

shirtless, luminous,
dark hair glowing in the warm,
grey room.

2.
Do you ever recall
the night I pulled you
out of the Afterlife?
No words exist
to explain the guttural sound
which woke me,

that alcoholic rattle
at three in the morning
which clattered from your throat

as we lay grounded, living within
our empty lives: a bare mattress
in a barren room.
Your body choked— wet with sweat
and bile—trying to spew
out the evening's alcohol,

to retch out life.
Yet you remained unconscious,
inert, not comprehending the full tide

of compensation left to pay back.
We transformed to an ugly pieta:
me supporting your holy head,

the naked body translated
to a new level, transported
to an aspect of divinity,

a new awareness—

3.
I never understood
why you wanted Death to rise
within your life, personified

as a trick in his late twenties.
Glassy-eyed. Coked up.
His right arm flicking ashes indifferently

as he lay next to you
in the dark, without emotion,
as he breathed in smoke,

considering the hairline cracks
running along the ceiling—
considering your t-cells spinning languidly

in thin-walled veins. Sometimes while you slept,
he would curl beside you, caress your forearm,
and tap inside the elbow to raise

the lines of green-blue channels,
to loosen out a casual
bruise for a matter of days.

He would watch it fade
from a dark violet to a sickly green.
Under half-closed lids,

his eyes measure
the distance of the future
from the edge of the bed.

4.
For a number of years
I had not dreamt of you.
Your ghost memory
avoided my room until
last autumn, when your body
was found as a moses-tongued swallow

trapped in a decaying house.
For me, your death remains
an unquiet frustration, a stone

cast between hands,
shifting back and forth,
restlessly. Agitated as a murder of crows
or a coven of ravens.
Remember how I once wrote
of feathers falling from your dark hair?

Every action from your comb
brushed out pinions, a collection of dark wings—
proof of actuality of your moment.

5.
As a mild bruising, forgiveness stains
within— spreads out,
rearranging impressions.

Or as uncertain stigmata,
discoloration left behind on bed sheets,
suggestions from past histories,

overt as cigarette burns and IV drips,
rusty blood pooling in small blotches,
the casual splurge of semen.

We carry these stains
within our lives
as a funerary shroud,

a coarse muslin,
wrapped closely against the skin,
as we step trembling

into the Afterworld.
Only I lied when I told you
that sins of the past were forgotten.

It is the same lie
I offer my son at night
rocking a sense of security

into his blood. The same lie
which repeats in my head at eventide,
when personal histories reel out slowly—

6.
Some stories are never resolved.
They spiral within themselves
in infinite loops of lost conversations—

some people clutch their denouements
tightly, as a clutch of dried flowers
or fading paper blossoms.

Like myself: it all falls back
to the beginning, the core memory
of you and I in side-street alleys,

between warehouse bars
by the riverfront, groping
to find the other's cannibalistic desire,

reaching within to pull forward
a sense of truth hidden
in the folds of damp clothing—

7.
Afterwards,
when you moved
from the waters of the Material World

and stood surrounded by hands
lifting you forward,
pulling you upwards,

was Ruth there as well to raise
your trembling into her fixed resolve?
I want to imagine her

supporting your coarse frame
drying off the slick waters
from your full body

from your fresh trembling
in the strange new air
of the Here After.

I see her paleness
slowly unknitting the threads
of what was left of your mortal coil,

bringing your essence
into an ever-changing light,
a light burning away all colors,

blurring individuality into
the new collective of awareness.
A soft rocking of assurance.

About the Author

Primarily a Poet and a Father of a young boy. Over the past fifteen years David-Glen Smith has served as an instructor, graphic designer, editor, and illustrator. His drawings and writings have been published in a variety of journals across the United States.

His influences range from early European folk-stories, the Magic Realist movement, and the Modernist movement. The verses in this collection contain changing rhythms and sporadic syllable counts. The manuscript displays the experience of a persona translating their personal experiences into surreal, dream-logic. On occasion, the writing moves in fragmented thoughts and blurring of personality patterns.

David's work has appeared in various magazines including most recently: *Assaracus, The Centrifugal Eye, ffrrfr, The Fertile Source, Houston Literary Review, Lady Jane Miscellany, Louisville Review, Mid-America Review, Melancholy Hyperbole, Saltwater Quarterly, Slant, The Steel-Toe Review*, and *The Write Room*. In addition, a recent print anthology titled *Ganymede—Unfinished* includes two of his poems.

Currently residing in Texas with his partner of over ten years, he teaches English Literature at both Wharton County Junior College and Lone Star College - CyFair. In 2010 they adopted a baby boy, Brendan—source of new material for poems!

David also serves as Editorial Assistant for the magazine *The Centrifugal Eye*. He holds an MFA from Vermont College, and a MA from the University of MO at St. Louis.

For more information visit: http://davidglensmith.blogspot.com/.

Acknowledgements

Many friends and mentors helped in the shaping of this book— from whom advice and encouragements should be acknowledged: Mark Doty, Lynda Hull, Susan Mitchell, Richard Jackson, Cyrus Cassells, and Joan Seliger Sidney— all in various ways helped untie many knots.

Keith Perilli deserves additional mention for his thought-provoking painting "Tread."

Likewise, before the poems existed in full form, there were other people who helped in many fashions: Bonnie and Lou Pfleckl, Melissa Marrs, Michaela Haberkern, Lynn Hall, the staff at *Left Bank Books,* and the late, frequently visited, *Duff's Restaurant* in the Central West End of Saint Louis.

Finally, a strong thanks needs to be delivered to Ron Starbuck and Saint Julian Press for final editing and proof of the text, building the manuscript into its present form, and answering numerous questions on my behalf.

Assaracus

>Listen
>Metamorphosis
>Metamorphosis: Ode to an Olympic Diver
>Metamorphosis: Ode to Kenny Fries

Ganymede—Unfinished
>Herakles Burning the Pyre

James White Review
>you, in darkness (xiii.)

Kestrel
>Herakles Crossing the River
>Herakles Wrestling with Death

Meadow
>Fragmented Still Life with Cardoon and Parsnips

Melancholy Hyperbole
    xii. I cannot justify my wanting you
    (published as "Found Fragment 1")
    xv. Some mornings, after an hour's run, after a slight
    (published as "Found Fragment 2")
    xviii. —the times I slept alone. Dreaming my slack
    (published as "Found Fragment 3")

Outerbridge
    Elegy for Gary

Notes

Section 1: Venerations of the Temple
• Twenty-Nine Reflections over the Remnants of a Codex
The codex described in the poem is imagined to be located in a hidden early cathedral somewhere in Ireland within the coastal counties. After a destructive fire struck the main library in 1432, a major portion of the parchment became damaged, and therefore illegible. Only fragments remain.

• Twenty-Six Verses from an Apocryphal Psalm
These scraps of verses were created a few weeks after the traumatic and irrational and unexplainable events at Newtown, CT.

• Saint Brendan and the Nordic Moon
It is related how Saint Brendan, the Navigator, discovered upper portions of the North American continent sometime eight hundred years before Christopher Columbus began his campaigns in Central America for the Spanish.

The moon in Nordic cultures was perceived as a masculine entity, whereas the sun was feminine.

• Saint Brendan Among Autumn Cypress
The Latin phrase appearing in section three comes directly from Psalm 51, verses 7-8, using the 1662 Book of Common Prayer translation:
Thou shalt purge me with hyssop, and I shall be clean: thou shalt wash me, and I shall be whiter than snow.
Thou shalt make me hear of joy and gladness: that the bones which thou hast broken may rejoice.

• An Untitled Poem for Beth
This poem uses two fractures of foreign language phrasings:
the German passage states "in Summer I think of you most often"
the Spanish passage states "with Spanish dialogues, / small revolutions, as the night / I watched your expressions / as we made love

Section 2: Variations of a Theme of Desire
These fragmented poems exist as a collection of deconstructed sonnets. The passages gathered display a scramble perspective of the persona's various relationships over the course of a series of years. The place names relate primarily with a region of Saint Louis, MO: the Central West End, where a

majority of the residential and commercial buildings date to the time of World's Fair of 1900.

• i. imitatio: a Classical practice of imitation, or emulation, by taking an original source and shifting it into something slightly other
• iii. Schiele: Egon Schiele (1890-1912) a celebrated Austrian painter whose Expressionist figure paintings translate the human body into elongated and emaciated forms.
• v. Diana: a reference to the Greco-Roman goddess of the hunt
• vi. for Phil Barron
• xi. nadamos en los ojos de dios: Spanish: "We swim in the eyes of God."
 tus manos: Spanish: "your hands"
• xv.   A casual reference to the poet Frank O'Hara (1926-1966): the postcard does exist.
• xii. Creve Coeur Park exists west of Saint Louis in a community known as Maryland Heights. Ironically, I discovered afterwards, the name is French for "Broken Heart."
• xvii.   Of the many stories which surround the classic Greek Herakles, one in particular mentions how in midst of his labors the hero burdened himself temporarily with the giant Atlas' task of keeping the weight of the heavens from touching the horizon line.
• xix.   Orpheus: a brief reference to the Greco-Roman tragic hero whose singing moved stones and the heart of Hades, the king of the Underworld.
• xx. Saint Louis woman...: the passage quoted derives from a Blues recording of "Saint Louis Blues" as sung by the legendary Bessie Smith.

Section 3: Metamorphosis
• Metamorphosis (i)
Horace: Roman lyric poet Quintus Horatius Flaccus (65 BCE – 8 BCE) is noted for his variety of Odes which celebrate everyday life and likewise contain a sense of political commentary.

• Herakles Wrestling with Death
It is recorded that on one of his many journeys, Herakles competed against the abstract entity of Thanatos as a favor for a friend for the life of a mortal Queen. This poem places the situation in a modern-like environment and re-examines the relationship between the two.

• Metamorphosis: Ode to Kenny Fries
This poem celebrates the contemporary poet Kenny Fries, reimagining him as Hesphaestus, Greek god of metalwork, fire, and armories.

• Metamorphosis: Ode to an Olympic Diver
Specifically, this work addresses Greg Louganis, Olympic Gold Medalist in 1984 and 1988.

• Herakles Burning the Pyre
At his death, the hero Herakles threw himself on his own funeral pyre, burning off his mortal body and sending his immortal divine essence to Olympus.

www.ingramcontent.com/pod-product-compliance
Lightning Source LLC
Chambersburg PA
CBHW020516100426
42813CB00030B/3262/J